Learning to read. Reading to learn!

LEVEL ONE Sounding It Out Preschool–Kindergarten
For kids who know their alphabet and are starting to sound out words.
   learning sight words • beginning reading • sounding out words

LEVEL TWO Reading with Help Preschool–Grade 1
For kids who know sight words and are learning to sound out new words.
   expanding vocabulary • building confidence • sounding out bigger words

LEVEL THREE Independent Reading Grades 1–3
For kids who are beginning to read on their own.
   introducing paragraphs • challenging vocabulary • reading for comprehension

LEVEL FOUR Chapters Grades 2–4
For confident readers who enjoy a mixture of images and story.
   reading for learning • more complex content • feeding curiosity

Ripley Readers Designed to help kids build their reading skills and confidence at any level, this program offers a variety of fun, entertaining, and unbelievable topics to interest even the most reluctant readers. With stories and information that will spark their curiosity, each book will motivate them to start and keep reading.

Vice President, Licensing & Publishing Amanda Joiner
Editorial Manager Carrie Bolin

Editor Jordie R. Orlando
Designer Luis Fuentes
Text Briana Posner
Reprographics Bob Prohaska

Chief Executive Officer Andy Edwards
Chief Commercial Officer Brett Clarke
Vice President, Global Licensing & Consumer Products Cassie Dombrowski
Vice President, Creative Dov Ribnik
Director, Brand & Athlete Marketing Ricky Melnik
Account Manager, Global Licensing & Consumer Products Andrew Hogan
Athlete Manager Chris Haffey

Published by Ripley Publishing 2020

10 9 8 7 6 5 4 3 2 1

Copyright © 2020 Nitro Circus

ISBN: 978-1-60991-399-1

No part of this publication may be reproduced in whole or in part, stored in a retrieval system, or transmitted in any form by any means, electronic, mechanical, photocopying, recording, or otherwise, without written permission from the publisher.

For more information regarding permission, contact:
VP Licensing & Publishing
Ripley Entertainment Inc.
7576 Kingspointe Parkway, Suite 188
Orlando, Florida 32819
Email: publishing@ripleys.com
www.ripleys.com/books

Manufactured in China in March 2020.

First Printing

Library of Congress Control Number: 2020931450

PUBLISHER'S NOTE
While every effort has been made to verify the accuracy of entries in this book, the Publisher cannot be held responsible for any errors contained in the work. They would be glad to receive any information from readers.

WARNING
Some of the stunts and activities are undertaken by experts and should not be attempted by anyone without adequate training and supervision.

PHOTO CREDITS

Cover Photography by Chris Tedesco **3** Photography by Chris Tedesco **4-5** Photography by Phil Lagettie **6** Photography by @nicolasjacquemin **8** Photography by Nate Christenson **9** Photography by Chris Ortiz **10** © JohnnyAsJack/Shutterstock.com **12-13** © lzf/Shutterstock.com **14** © Nataliia Zhekova/Shutterstock.com **15** Photography by Chris Wellhausen **19** Photography by Chris Wellhausen **20** Photography by Chris Wellhausen **22** Photography by Sport the library/Courtney Crow **23** Photography by Chris Tedesco **25** Photography by Sport the library/Jeff Crow **26-27** Sean M. Haffey/Getty Images **28-29** Photography by Chris Ortiz **30-31** © FiledIMAGE/Shutterstock.com

All other photos are courtesy of Nitro Circus. Every attempt has been made to acknowledge correctly and contact copyright holders, and we apologize in advance for any unintentional errors or omissions, which will be corrected in future editions.

LEXILE®, LEXILE FRAMEWORK®, LEXILE ANALYZER®, the LEXILE® logo and POWERV® are trademarks of MetaMetrics, Inc., and are registered in the United States and abroad. The trademarks and names of other companies and products mentioned herein are the property of their respective owners. Copyright © 2020 MetaMetrics, Inc. All rights reserved.

SKATEBOARDING!

Nitro Circus is a group of men and women who perform stunts.

They love skateboards!

They do lots of tricks when they ride.

A skateboard has four wheels.

Riders use one foot to push the skateboard.

They use the other
foot to balance.

You can ride skateboards on the street.

Most ride in parks.

Riders use helmets to stay safe.

They also use pads.

Some kids compete in
the Nitro Junior Games.

They can show off their skills.

The Nitro Circus riders go down big ramps!

They jump high!

The riders can even do flips.

Who will do the best trick?

That's so cool!

Skateboards are so much fun!

Ripley Readers

Ready for More?

GO BIG!

Pushing the limits and breaking boundaries in action sports.

From BMX to FMX and everything in between—including skateboards, scooters, and crazy contraptions—dive into all things Nitro Circus! You'll read about the equipment, the amazing athletes, unbelievable tricks, and more! Ripley Level 2 Readers are perfect for kids who know their sight words and are learning to sound out new words.

Learning to read. Reading to learn!

Reading With Help
Preschool-Grade 1
- expanding vocabulary
- building confidence
- sounding out bigger words

Independent Reading
Grades 1-3
- introducing paragraphs
- challenging vocabulary
- reading for comprehension

For more information about Ripley's Believe It or Not!, go to www.ripleys.com